Cooking Alaska's Wild Salmon

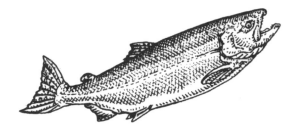

By Kathy Doogan

Illustrations by Ray Troll

Alaska
Cook Book Co.
Anchorage

Cooking Alaska's Wild Salmon

Distributed by

Todd Communications
611 E. 12th Ave.
Anchorage, Alaska 99501-4603 U.S.A.
Telephone: **(907) 274-TODD (8633)**
Telefax: (907) 929-5550
Sales@toddcom.com
WWW.ALASKABOOKSANDCALENDARS.COM

With other offices and warehouses in:
Ketchikan, Juneau, Fairbanks and Nome, Alaska

**Written, edited and designed by
Kathy Doogan / Raven Design**

Artwork © Ray Troll, 2009

First Printing January, 2010

ISBN: 978-1-57833-475-9

Printed by Everbest Printing, Co., Ltd., Nansha, China
through **Alaska Print Brokers**, Anchorage, Alaska.

Additional copies of this book may be ordered directly from the distributor
for US $19.95 (includes US $6.00 postage & handling).

On the cover: Midnight Run, © Ray Troll, 2009

Contents

Acknowledgements

When I started looking for cooks to help me test the recipes in this book, I was surprised and gratified to receive such an enthusiastic response from my friends. I am indebted to the following group of now-expert recipe testers, each of whom wholeheartedly embraced the project: Heather Beaty, Cass Crandall, RuthAnn Dickie, Barbara Doogan, Kayla Epstein, Krissy Gable, JoAnn Grady, Davida Kapler, Katie Koester, Rosanne Pagano and Tina Seaton. They're all great cooks and provided countless suggestions and comments that made the recipes better. All have earned my undying gratitude.

My thanks also go to Ray Troll, whose artwork has added just the right touch of whimsy to these pages; to Laura Fleming of the Alaska Seafood Marketing Institute (ASMI) for her valuable help with the general information section of this book; to Amy Doogan for the thorough job she did catching my mistakes; and to talented Alaska chefs Patrick Hoogerhyde (Glacier Brewhouse), Brett Knipmeyer (Kinley's Restaurant), Al Levinsohn (Kincaid Grill) and Justin Persons (Double Musky Inn) for sharing some of their favorite salmon recipes.

Finally, I'd like to thank my husband, Mike, for all the times he politely kept his mouth shut when the answer to his question, "What's for dinner?" was, once again, "Salmon."

— *Kathy Doogan*

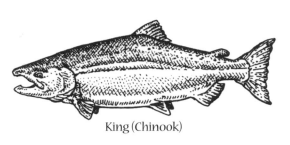

King (Chinook)

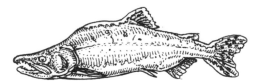

Red (Sockeye)

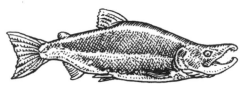

Silver (Coho)

Pink (Humpback)

Chum (Dog)

RAY TROLL 2008

Introduction

Wild Alaska Salmon

The waters in and around Alaska are home to five species of wild salmon, each of which is prized for its unique flavor and texture.

King (Chinook) salmon, the largest, least abundant and most expensive salmon, can weigh from 4 to 50 pounds. Kings, considered by many to be the premier Alaska salmon, have a high oil content and firm-textured, bright orange flesh. (A small number have white or marbled flesh, natural genetic variations.)

Red (Sockeye) salmon are the second most abundant salmon in Alaska waters and have deep red flesh and a rich flavor, making them a favorite for cooking fresh and canning. Red salmon commonly weigh 4 to 8 pounds.

Coho (Silver) salmon weigh from 8 to 12 pounds and have orange-red flesh and a firm texture that holds up well to freezing.

Pink (Humpback) salmon, the most abundant and economical of the species, are known for their light pink flesh and delicate flavor. Pinks, with an average weight of 3 to 4 pounds, have the lowest fat content of the five types of Alaska salmon, making them a good choice for canning or serving with sauces.

Chum (Dog) salmon are most often used for drying or smoking. They have a weight range of 7 to 18 pounds, orange-pink flesh and a low fat content.

Wild Alaska salmon is considered by cooks and consumers to be the highest-quality salmon in the world. Like other wild salmon, Alaska salmon are born in fresh water, live the majority of their lives in the ocean, then return to the freshwater stream where they were born to spawn and then die. (Scientists have studied salmon to try to determine how they are able to return to the exact location of their birth, but there has been no definitive explanation for how this lifetime memory works.) How far the salmon have to travel to their spawning grounds determines how much fat the fish must store for the journey. In turn, the fish's fat content is what provides its delicate flavor.

Nutritional Information

Wild Alaska salmon is a nutritional powerhouse. In addition to being an excellent source of high-quality, easily-digestible protein, fresh salmon contains vitamins A, B6, B12 and E, as well as thiamin, niacin, riboflavin, panothenic acid, phosphorus, potassium, selenium and heart-healthy Omega-3 fish oil. Canned salmon (with bones) also contains significant amounts of vitamin D and calcium.

For these reasons, medical experts agree that eating salmon is important to a healthy diet, and that it can decrease the risk of heart disease and some cancers.

Much more information about wild Alaska salmon, including resource management, fishing and processing methods and sustainability of the resource is available from the Alaska Seafood Marketing Institute (*www.alaskaseafood.org*).

A Word About Farmed Salmon

Although wild Alaska salmon is widely available throughout the country, consumers outside Alaska might find another salmon in their markets — farmed Atlantic salmon. Much has been written about the environmental and health concerns surrounding farmed salmon. More information on these issues is available from many organizations involved in seafood safety, such as the Monterey Bay Aquarium's Seafood Watch program (*www.seafoodwatch.org*). Nutritionally, farmed salmon is somewhat similar to wild salmon, however, from a culinary standpoint, the meat of farmed salmon is oilier and has a softer texture than wild fish.

Notes on the Recipes in this Book

Many of the recipes that follow call for cooked salmon in some form. Some recipes specify canned salmon, some call for fresh, cooked fish. In reality, the type of salmon used is interchangeable. As long as you have the amount of fish needed for the recipe, it doesn't matter if the fish is canned or fresh.

For recipes using cooked salmon, a few helpful equivalents are:

1 pound raw salmon fillet (skin on) =
about 2 cups cooked salmon, skin and bones removed

1 small can of salmon (7 to 8 ounces) =
a scant 1 cup of salmon after draining well

1 large can of salmon (14 to 15 ounces) =
about 1 3/4 cups of salmon after draining well

Removing the skin and bones from canned salmon is a purely aesthetic decision. Both can be safely eaten and, in fact, the bones in canned salmon contribute significant amounts of calcium.

Smoked salmon comes in two main types. Hot-smoked salmon is cooked, and is usually sold as fillets and sometimes called wood-smoked or kippered salmon. Cold-smoked salmon, which is uncooked and is translucent in appearance, is most often sold as lox or gravlax. Cold-smoked salmon is typically eaten as is and is seldom used in cooking. The recipes in this book which call for smoked salmon are intended for the hot-smoked type of fish.

And finally, unless you've done it many times, removing the skin from a raw salmon fillet can be a little tricky. The easiest way to do it is to ask your butcher to remove the skin for you. If that's not an option, search "removing salmon skin" on the internet — you'll find many videos showing you how to do it yourself.

— *Kathy Doogan*

Appetizers

Phyllis' Smoked Salmon Ball

This recipe originally came from my mother's cousin, Phyllis, who always loved a party.

> 1 small can (7 to 8 ounces) salmon, drained, skin and bones removed if desired
> 8 ounces cream cheese, softened
> $1/2$ teaspoon prepared horseradish (or more to taste)
> $1/8$ to $1/4$ teaspoon Liquid Smoke (see note)
> 1 tablespoon grated onion
> 1 teaspoon lemon juice
> $1/3$ cup pecans, finely chopped
> 2 tablespoons parsley, finely chopped

In a medium bowl, mix salmon, cream cheese, horseradish, Liquid Smoke, onion and lemon juice. Stir until well combined then chill until mixture sets up (at least an hour).

Spread pecans and parsley on a sheet of waxed paper. Form the salmon mixture into a ball and roll in pecans and parsley to cover completely. Place on a serving dish and refrigerate until ready to serve. Serve with crackers or thin slices of French bread baguettes.

NOTE: Liquid Smoke is a very concentrated ingredient. Use care when measuring as even a little too much can spoil your recipe. It's best to start with the smallest amount and add more to taste.

Smoked Salmon Spread

    1 large package cream cheese (8 ounces) softened
    3 tablespoons half-and-half or cream
    1 tablespoon lemon juice
    2 teaspoons chives or fresh dill, finely minced
    1 cup finely chopped smoked salmon (about 5 or 6 ounces),
        skin and bones removed before chopping

Whisk the cream cheese, half-and-half, lemon juice and chives or dill until smooth. Fold in the salmon. Spoon into a serving bowl and chill at least an hour. Serve with crackers.

Makes about 2 cups

Smoked Salmon Puffs

    1 recipe Smoked Salmon Spread (above)
    24 to 36 butter crackers, such as Ritz, or Melba rounds

Preheat broiler.

Mound a rounded teaspoonful of the Smoked Salmon Spread onto each cracker. Place crackers on a baking sheet and broil briefly until salmon mixture starts to bubble (watch closely, this only takes a minute or two). Serve immediately.

Makes 2 to 3 dozen appetizers

Eight Layer Salmon Dip

1 tablespoon vegetable oil
2 cups cooked salmon (about 1 pound), skin and bones
   removed and flaked with fork
1 tablespoon chili powder, divided
1 can (15 ounces) regular or fat-free refried beans
1 bunch green onions, thinly sliced
1 medium can (about 4 ounces) sliced black olives, drained
2 ripe avocados
1 tablespoon lime juice
2 cups chunky salsa, any type
2 cups (16 ounces) sour cream
2 cups shredded Cheddar or Monterey Jack cheese
1 large bag tortilla chips

Heat vegetable oil in a non-stick skillet over medium-high heat. Add salmon and sprinkle with 2 teaspoons of chili powder. Heat quickly, stirring constantly, until salmon is warm and evenly seasoned. Set aside to cool slightly.

Warm the refried beans on the stove or in the microwave. Stir in 1 teaspoon of chili powder and spoon the mixture into the bottom of a large, shallow serving bowl. Top the beans with the sliced green onions, then the olives.

Peel, seed and dice avocados. Toss avocados with lime juice then spoon them in a layer on top of the olives. Top with salsa, spread sour cream over salsa, then finish with a layer of cheese.

Serve with tortilla chips.

Smoked Salmon Cheesecake Squares

6 tablespoons butter, divided
1 cup bread crumbs
1 ¼ cups (about 4 ounces) finely grated Swiss or Gruyère
   cheese, divided
3 teaspoons minced fresh dill, divided
1 medium onion, finely chopped
3 large (8 ounces each) packages cream cheese, softened
   (do not use lowfat or nonfat)
4 large eggs
½ cup half-and-half
1 ½ cups (about 8 ounces) coarsely chopped smoked
   salmon, skin and bones removed
½ cup sour cream (for garnish)

Preheat oven to 350°F.

Line a 9" by 13" baking pan with aluminum foil, making sure the
foil is long enough to come up and over the sides for easy removal
later. Generously butter (about 2 tablespoons) the bottom and
sides of the foil lining.

Over low heat, melt 2 tablespoons of butter in a medium skillet;
stir in the bread crumbs. Remove from heat and mix in ½ cup
of the cheese and 1 teaspoon of the minced dill. Press mixture
evenly into the bottom of the prepared pan. Bake crust for 10 to 12
minutes, until just starting to brown. Remove from oven and cool.

Return skillet to stove and melt the remaining 2 tablespoons of
butter over medium heat. Add the onion and cook, stirring often,
until soft (do not brown), about 10 minutes.

In a food processor or blender, process the cream cheese until
smooth. Add eggs, remaining ¾ cup of cheese and the half-and-
half and mix until smooth, stopping once to scrape down the sides
of the work bowl. Add the sautéed onions and the salmon and
pulse once or twice, just to mix. Do not overmix.

(continued on next page)

Pour the filling over the crust and place the pan on a baking sheet. Bake for 50 to 60 minutes (center of cheesecake should be firm to the touch). When cheesecake is done, turn the oven off and leave the cheesecake in the oven to cool for about 1 hour with the door slightly ajar. Remove the pan from the oven, let it cool to room temperature, then cover with plastic wrap and chill.

To serve, carefully lift the edges of the foil from the pan and peel from the sides of the cheesecake. Cut into small (about 1 ½") squares and arrange on a large plate. Top each square with a small dab of sour cream and a tiny pinch of the remaining minced dill. Can be served chilled or at room temperature.

Makes about 48 appetizers

Smoked Salmon Cupcakes

    1 cup all-purpose flour
    2 teaspoons baking powder
    2 tablespoons finely minced chives
    $\frac{1}{2}$ cup (1 stick) butter or margarine, melted
    $\frac{1}{2}$ cup sour cream (do not use lowfat or nonfat)
    $\frac{1}{3}$ cup (about 2 ounces) finely chopped smoked salmon,
       skin and bones removed before chopping
    Lemon Cream Cheese (recipe follows)

Preheat oven to 350°F.

Place flour, baking powder and chives in bowl and stir to combine. Mix in melted butter or margarine, sour cream and salmon, stirring until well combined (dough will be stiff). Scoop one slightly rounded measuring tablespoon of dough into each cup of an ungreased mini-muffin tin (1¾" diameter). Use your finger to smooth the tops, then place the tin in the oven and bake for 20 to 25 minutes, until light golden brown and cooked through. Let tins cool on a rack for about 5 minutes, then remove cupcakes and cool completely before "frosting" with Lemon Cream Cheese.

Lemon Cream Cheese

    3 ounces cream cheese, softened to room temperature
    2 tablespoons sour cream
    1 tablespoon lemon juice
    1 tablespoon minced chives
    2 tablespoons salmon caviar (optional)

Combine softened cream cheese, sour cream and lemon juice in a small bowl, stirring until mixture is smooth and of spreading consistency (add more sour cream if needed). Frost cupcakes and decorate with chive "sprinkles" and salmon caviar. If not serving immediately, refrigerate. Bring to room temperature before serving.

Makes 24 cupcakes

Smoked Salmon Stuffed Potatoes

4 ounces smoked salmon, finely chopped (about 3/4 cup)
2 tablespoons sour cream
2 tablespoons mayonnaise
1 tablespoon capers, drained and chopped
1/4 teaspoon black pepper
1/2 teaspoon prepared white horseradish
12 small red-skinned potatoes (about the size of a golf ball)
1 tablespoon finely chopped chives

Mix the salmon, sour cream, mayonnaise, capers, salt, pepper and horseradish in a small bowl. Cover and chill. (Salmon mixture can be made one day ahead.)

Place the potatoes in a medium saucepan and cover with water. Bring to a boil and cook until soft when pierced in the center, about 10 to 12 minutes. Drain and place potatoes on a rack to cool.

When potatoes are cool enough to handle, cut them in half, then cut a thin slice off the rounded end (bottom) of each potato half so it will sit upright. Using a melon baller, small spoon or paring knife, take a small scoop out of the cut side (top) of each potato, creating a small potato "cup." Coarsely chop the removed scoops of potato and add to the salmon mixture. Mix well, adding additional mayonnaise if mixture is too dry.

Fill each potato cup with a rounded spoonful of filling and garnish with a small pinch of chives. Refrigerate if not serving immediately.

Makes 24 appetizers

Salmon Gravlax

> 1 cup coarse Kosher salt
> ½ cup sugar
> 1 tablespoon whole black peppercorns
> 1 pound salmon fillet, previously frozen (see caution below),
>   about 1" thick (center cut if possible), bones removed
> 2 tablespoons gin or vodka (optional)
> 1 small bunch fresh dill

In a small bowl, mix the salt, sugar and black peppercorns.

Place the salmon fillet, skin side down, on a piece of plastic wrap about 3 times as long as the fillet. Spread the salt mixture on top of the fish, pressing it gently with your hands (be sure the salt covers the fish completely so that no part of it is exposed). If using, sprinkle the gin or vodka over the salt. Evenly spread the dill over the top. Wrap the salmon tightly in the plastic wrap and place it in a shallow glass dish. Place a smaller dish or pan on top of the fish and add weight (several unopened cans of soup or beans work well).

Place in the refrigerator for about 24 to 48 hours, during which time the fish will give off some liquid and will become semi-opaque and somewhat rigid. Open the package and scrape off the dill and salt mixture completely with a large spoon. Wipe the fish with paper towels to remove any remaining salt mixture. If desired, the fish may be rinsed under cold water, then dried thoroughly before serving.

To serve, slice thinly on a slight diagonal, holding the knife at a 15- to 20-degree angle. Gravlax is traditionally served with bagels or dark brown bread and cream cheese, capers and chopped red onion. The fish should keep up to 2 weeks, well wrapped and refrigerated.

Makes about 1 pound

Raw fish safety caution: *Because wild salmon may be infected with parasites, the U.S. Food and Drug Administration (FDA) recommends that fish to be consumed raw should be frozen at -35°C (-31°F) for 15 hours, or at -20°C (-4°F) for 7 days before it can be considered safe. (Brining and pickling may reduce the hazard, but not to a safe level.) Most home freezers do not get cold enough to comply with FDA guidelines, so when eating wild salmon raw or rare, purchase fish that has been commercially frozen.*

Asian Salmon Tartar

Please see the raw fish safety caution on the previous page.

> 2 tablespoons extra virgin olive oil
> 1 tablespoons sesame oil
> 2 teaspoons grated fresh ginger
> 2 teaspoons soy sauce
> 1/4 teaspoon pepper
> 1/2 pound to 3/4 pound salmon fillet (preferably king), cut
>   into cubes about 1/4" (skin and bones removed)
> 1 medium shallot, finely chopped
> 1/2 cup peeled, seeded and finely diced cucumber
> 1 tablespoon finely chopped cilantro

Combine olive oil, sesame oil, ginger, soy sauce and pepper in a small bowl. Whisk to combine well.

Place salmon, shallot, cucumber and cilantro in a serving bowl. Pour dressing over and stir gently until well combined. Cover and refrigerate at least an hour. Before serving, stir and pour off any accumulated liquid.

Serve ice cold with small, thin slices of toasted bread.

Makes 4 appetizer servings

Double Musky's Coconut Salmon

Chef Justin Persons
Double Musky Inn, Girdwood

Beer Batter (recipe follows)
1 pound salmon, skin removed
2 cups shredded coconut
Oil (enough to be at least 3" deep in frying pot)
Sweet and Sour Sauce (recipe follows)

Prepare beer batter and refrigerate until ready to use.

Cut salmon into squares 2" long by 2" wide and ½" thick.
(At the restaurant, we use trimmings from the fillets we use
for other dishes, as can you. They don't have to be perfectly
uniform).

Using a strainer, shake coconut well so that most of the sugar
is shaken off. Dip salmon pieces into beer batter, then quickly
but thoroughly coat with coconut.

Heat oil in a deep fat fryer to 375°F. (If you don't have a frying
thermometer, a good way to tell when the oil is hot enough is
to drop in a thin slice of scallion — if it immediately begins to
spin, the oil is ready.)

Carefully place fish into the hot oil and fry until salmon pieces
turn dark brown but are not burned. Drain on paper towels to
absorb excess oil.

Serve with Sweet and Sour Sauce. The fried salmon is best
eaten immediately.

Serves 2

Beer Batter

1 cup beer (open and let the beer go flat in the
    refrigerator overnight)
2 tablespoons vegetable oil
2 eggs
$3/4$ teaspoon salt
Dash of black pepper
1 $1/2$ teaspoons granulated garlic or garlic powder
$3/4$ cup water
2 $3/4$ cups flour

Mix together all of the ingredients except the flour (if you use garlic powder instead of granulated garlic, mix it in with the flour instead to avoid clumps). Add most of the flour and mix well. Add remaining flour until desired consistency is reached (much like pancake batter). Refrigerate until ready to use.

Sweet and Sour Sauce

1 $1/2$ cups grape jelly
$1/2$ cup Dijon mustard
1 $1/2$ teaspoons prepared horseradish

Melt the grape jelly in a saucepan over low heat, stirring occasionally, until the lumps have dissolved. Stir in the mustard and horseradish; cool then chill. Serve cold. Makes 2 cups.

Brunches & Lunches

Creamed Salmon on Toast

Here's a simple and quick lunch or light dinner for one of those days when you need to make a meal from what you have in the pantry. The recipe can be easily doubled.

    3 tablespoons butter or margarine
    3 tablespoons flour
    2 cups milk
    $1/2$ teaspoon salt
    $1/4$ teaspoon black pepper
    1 small can salmon (7 to 8 ounces), drained well, skin and bones removed if desired
    2 large eggs, hardboiled, peeled and coarsely chopped
    $1/2$ cup frozen peas, thawed (optional)
    4 slices of bread, toasted and buttered

Melt butter or margarine in a medium saucepan and stir in flour. Cook for 1 to 2 minutes, then slowly add milk. Cook, stirring often, until mixture thickens and almost comes to a boil. Reduce heat to low, add salt and pepper and gently stir in salmon, eggs and peas (if using). Continue to cook for 2 or 3 minutes, until all ingredients are heated through.

To serve, spoon over buttered toast.

Serves 2

Baked Salmon Frittata

3 tablespoons vegetable oil
1 large potato (about 1 pound), peeled and cut into 1/2" cubes
1/2 cup diced red or yellow onion
1/2 cup diced red or yellow bell pepper
1 clove garlic, minced or pressed
1 large can salmon (15 to 16 ounces), drained, or 1 1/2 to 2 cups
   cooked salmon, skin and bones removed
3/4 cup cherry tomatoes, quartered and drained on paper
   towels
6 large eggs, beaten well
1/2 cup milk
3 tablespoons chopped fresh cilantro, divided
1 teaspoon salt
1/4 teaspoon black pepper
1 cup white cheese (such as Monterey Jack), shredded

Preheat oven to 400°F.

Heat oil in frying pan over medium heat. Add potato, onion and
bell pepper. Cook for about 5 minutes, until onion begins to soften;
stir in garlic and continue cooking for another 2 to 3 minutes until
potatoes are browned and almost cooked. Spoon potato mixture into
a greased 9" square baking dish. Break up salmon with a fork and
scatter it and the tomatoes on top of the potato mixture.

In a small bowl, blend eggs, milk, 2 tablespoons of the cilantro and
the salt and pepper; pour over salmon. Place frittata in oven and
bake for about 15 minutes. Sprinkle cheese on top and continue
baking for 8 to 10 minutes, until puffy and eggs are cooked through
(center of frittata should be firm). Remove from oven and allow to
rest for 10 to 15 minutes before cutting. Sprinkle remaining cilantro
on top and serve.

Serves 4 to 6

Salmon Hash

1 tablespoon butter
2 tablespoons vegetable oil
1 large potato (about 1 pound), peeled and cut into ½" cubes
½ cup onion, coarsely chopped
½ cup diced red bell pepper
½ cup diced green pepper
1½ to 2 cups cooked salmon (skin and bones removed),
   flaked with fork
½ teaspoon salt
½ teaspoon pepper
2 to 3 large eggs, poached (optional)

Heat butter and vegetable oil in a large nonstick skillet over medium-high heat. Add potatoes and cook, stirring often, until potatoes are almost done and turning golden brown (8 to 10 minutes). Stir in onions and peppers and continue cooking until vegetables are soft, about 5 minutes longer. Add salmon, salt and pepper; stir to combine then cook without stirring until bottom begins to brown and develop a crust. Carefully turn hash with a spatula and cook the other side until it gets brown and crusty, pressing down on the mixture with your spatula to make sure it makes good contact with the bottom of the pan.

Top each serving with a poached egg, if desired.

Serves 2 to 3

Smoked Salmon Pizza

1 medium yellow onion, peeled and thinly sliced into rings
3 tablespoons olive oil, divided
½ cup white wine or chicken or vegetable broth
1 tablespoon parsley, chopped
8 ounces smoked salmon (about 1 cup), skin and bones
    removed
1 large clove garlic, minced or pressed
12" prebaked pizza crust (such as Boboli®), regular or thin
½ green bell pepper, cut into thin slices OR 6 to 8 spears of
    fresh asparagus
1 cup shredded mozarella cheese

Preheat oven to 450°F. Place oven rack in lower third of oven.

In a skillet over medium high heat, sauté onions in 2 tablespoons
of olive oil until soft. Lower heat to medium, then add wine or
broth and continue to cook until most of the liquid is evaporated,
stirring occasionally. Remove pan from heat and stir in parsley and
smoked salmon, breaking it up with a fork.

In a small bowl, mix 1 remaining tablespoon of olive oil with the
minced garlic and brush onto the crust. Top with the salmon
mixture, spreading it out to the edges of the crust. Arrange green
pepper strips or asparagus spears on crust then top with shredded
cheese. Transfer pizza to a baking sheet and bake 8 to 10 minutes,
until cheese is melted and bubbly. Allow to cool slightly before
cutting.

Serves 2 to 3

Alaska Salmon Burgers

1 ½ to 2 pounds salmon fillet (skin and bones removed),
   cut into ¼" to ½" cubes
1 egg white, beaten
¼ cup fine bread crumbs
1 clove garlic, minced or pressed
2 tablespoons bottled barbeque sauce
½ teaspoon salt
¼ teaspoon pepper
1 tablespoon vegetable oil
4 slices Monterey Jack or Pepper Jack cheese (optional)
4 hamburger buns or Kaiser rolls, split
Sliced tomato
Sliced red onion
Sliced dill pickles
Shredded lettuce

In a medium bowl, mix salmon cubes with egg white, bread crumbs, garlic, barbeque sauce, salt and pepper. Refrigerate for at least 30 minutes or up to 2 hours.

Form salmon mixture into 4 evenly sized patties. Heat oil in a large skillet over medium-high heat. Add patties, lower heat to medium and cook for about 4 to 5 minutes. Carefully turn salmon over and cook for another 4 to 5 minutes or until just done in center (test with a knife). If using cheese, top patties with cheese slices for the last 2 or 3 minutes of cooking.

To serve, place each salmon burger on a bun. Top with tomato, onion, pickles and lettuce as desired.

Serves 4

Salmon Pocket Pies

This recipe is great for when you have just a little leftover salmon to use up.

> 1 cup cooked salmon, skin and bones removed
>   (about 1/2 pound)
> 3/4 cup cooked rice or finely chopped cooked potato
> 1/4 cup sliced green onions
> 1/4 cup diced red bell pepper
> 2 tablespoons mayonnaise
> 1 tablespoon chopped fresh parsley or 1 teaspoon dried
>   parsley
> 2 teaspoons fresh lemon juice
> 1/4 teaspoon garlic powder
> 1/4 teaspoon salt
> 1/4 teaspoon black pepper
> 1 package (8 ounces) refrigerated crescent rolls

Preheat oven to 350°F.

In a large bowl, combine salmon, rice or potato, green onions, red bell pepper, mayonnaise, parsley, lemon juice, garlic powder, salt and pepper. Gently stir until thoroughly mixed.

Open refrigerated rolls and separate dough into 4 rectangles (each will be made up of 2 triangles). Working with one rectangle at a time, place on a lightly floured board and roll the rectangle into a 6" to 7" square (be sure the perforation between the triangles is sealed). Place one-fourth of the filling mixture near one corner of the dough (leave a 1" border around the edges). Fold the opposite corner over to form a triangle; press the edges together with a fork to seal completely. Repeat process with remaining dough and filling to make 4 pies.

Place pocket pies on an ungreased baking sheet and bake for 15 to 20 minutes, until golden brown. Cool slightly before serving.

Serves 2 to 4

Salmon Pita Sandwiches

> 2 cups cooked salmon or 1 large can (14 to 15 ounces) salmon,
>   skin and bones removed
> ½ cup grated Cheddar cheese
> ½ cup thinly sliced celery
> ½ cup shredded carrot
> ½ cup diced onion
> ¼ cup sliced black or green olives
> ½ cup mayonnaise
> 2 tablespoons bottled Ranch salad dressing
> 4 pita breads
> 4 large lettuce leaves
> 1 large tomato, thinly sliced

In a large bowl, flake salmon with a fork then add Cheddar, celery, carrot, onion and olives; stir just to combine. Using a spoon or large fork, stir in mayonnaise and Ranch dressing and mix until all ingredients are well combined.

Cut a slice off the top of each pita and open the pocket. Line each pita with a lettuce leaf, add sliced tomato then spoon in the salmon filling.

Serves 4

Southwest Salmon Pitas

Prepare Salmon Pita filling as above with the following changes: Substitute diced red bell pepper for the carrot, use spicy salsa in place of the Ranch dressing, and add 2 tablespoons chopped cilantro to the salmon mixture. Proceed to fill the pitas as detailed above.

Serves 4

Salmon Stuffed Tomatoes with Basil Vinaigrette

2 large, ripe tomatoes
1/4 cup olive oil
1 tablespoon balsamic vinegar
1 tablespoon finely grated Parmesan cheese
1 tablespoon finely minced fresh basil
1 medium clove of garlic, minced or pressed
1/2 teaspoon salt
1/4 teaspoon pepper
1 1/2 cups cooked salmon (about 3/4 pound), skin and bones
    removed
1 small rib of celery, thinly sliced
1 medium avocado, peeled and diced

Cut tomatoes in half crosswise and carefully scoop out flesh and seeds with a small spoon. Turn tomato halves over on paper towels and allow them to drain while you make the dressing and the stuffing.

In a small bowl, make dressing by whisking together olive oil, vinegar, Parmesan, basil, garlic, salt, and pepper. Set aside.

In a separate bowl, crumble salmon with your fingers; add celery and avocado. Pour on dressing and toss gently to combine. Mound the salmon mixture into the four prepared tomato halves and serve.

Serves 2

Salmon Salad Wraps

> 2 cups cooked salmon (about 1 pound), skin and bones
>   removed
> 8 ounces softened regular or lowfat cream cheese
> 3 tablespoons finely chopped red onion
> 1 tablespoon lemon juice
> 1 teaspoon salt
> 2 tablespoons chopped cilantro or flatleaf parsley
> 4 large (10", burrito size) flour tortillas
> 4 large lettuce leaves, center ribs removed, or 2 cups
>   shredded lettuce
> 1/2 cup shredded carrots
> 1 cup alfalfa sprouts (optional)
> 1 cup seeded and chopped tomato

In a medium bowl, thoroughly combine salmon, cream cheese, onion, lemon juice, salt and cilantro or parsley.

Place tortillas on work surface. Spread each with one fourth of the salmon-cream cheese mixture, leaving a 1/2" edge all around. Place a lettuce leaf (or spread 1/2 cup shredded lettuce) over each tortilla, then put equal amounts of carrots, sprouts (if using) and chopped tomato down the center of each. Fold the sides over about 1" then roll up each tortilla like a burrito and cut it diagonally into 2 pieces.

Serves 4

Grilled King Salmon on Tasso Ham Cornbread

Chef Brett Knipmeyer
Kinley's Restaurant, Anchorage

Fresh Alaskan king salmon (about 6 ounces per portion)
Blueberry Barbeque Sauce (recipe follows)
Tasso Ham Cornbread (recipe follows)
Fresh blueberries for garnish (optional)

Grill salmon with skin side down first and then on other side. Be sure to get good grill marks and turn often to ensure fish is cooked to desired doneness.

To serve: Using a large (at least 3") biscuit cutter, cut a round of cornbread, lean salmon up against it, and serve with Blueberry Barbeque Sauce. Garnish with fresh blueberries if available.

Blueberry Barbeque Sauce

2 teaspoons vegetable oil
$1/2$ cup diced onions
1 tablespoon chopped garlic
6 tablespoons red wine vinegar
2 tablespoons brown sugar
2 tablespoons honey
$1/2$ cup beef stock
$2/3$ cup ketchup
1 tablespoon dry mustard
1 tablespoon Worcestershire sauce
2 cups frozen blueberries

In a large saucepan, heat vegetable oil over medium-low heat. Add onions and cook slowly until soft, about 5 minutes. Do not brown. Add remaining ingredients, raise heat and bring just to a boil. Lower heat and simmer for 30 minutes.

Tasso Ham Cornbread

  2 tablespoons vegetable oil
  1 yellow onion, diced
  $^1/_2$ cup red bell pepper, diced
  $^1/_2$ cup yellow bell pepper, diced
  $^1/_2$ cup green bell pepper, diced
  $^1/_2$ pound Tasso Ham, diced (see note)
  1 $^1/_4$ cups yellow cornmeal
  1 $^1/_2$ cups all-purpose flour
  $^3/_4$ cup sugar
  2 teaspoons baking powder
  $^1/_2$ teaspoon baking soda
  $^1/_2$ teaspoon salt
  1 $^1/_2$ cups buttermilk
  3 large eggs
  6 tablespoons butter, melted

Preheat oven to 350°F. Grease a 9" by 13" baking pan.

Heat vegetable oil in a large skillet over medium-low heat. Add onions and peppers and cook until soft, about 10 minutes. Remove from heat and cool.

In a large mixing bowl, combine ham, cornmeal, flour, sugar, baking powder, baking soda and salt. In a separate bowl, combine buttermilk, eggs, melted butter and cooled vegetables. Pour this mixture into the dry ingredients and stir just until combined. Do not overmix – some lumps are okay. Pour batter into prepared baking pan and bake 20 to 25 minutes, or until golden brown and still moist in center (do not overbake).

NOTE: Tasso ham is a spicy ham used in Cajun cooking. If you can't find it, Andouille or any other spicy sausage can be substituted. It should be cooked before adding to the batter.

Salads & Soups

Smoked Salmon Pasta Salad

$1/4$ cup extra virgin olive oil
2 tablespoons mayonnaise
1 tablespoon Dijon mustard
1 tablespoon balsamic or red wine vinegar
1 large clove garlic, minced or pressed
$1/2$ teaspoon salt
$1/4$ teaspoon black pepper
8 ounces rotini or fusilli (corkscrew) pasta
$1/2$ cup red onion, diced
$1/2$ cup celery, diced
$1/2$ cup red or yellow bell pepper, diced
3 tablespoons capers, drained and coarsely chopped
$1/4$ cup shredded Parmesan cheese
4 to 6 ounces smoked salmon, chopped (about $1/2$ cup)
2 tablespoons pine nuts, toasted briefly over medium heat
   in a dry skillet (optional)

Make dressing by combining olive oil, mayonnaise, mustard, vinegar, garlic, salt and pepper in a small bowl; whisk until smooth. Cover and chill.

Cook pasta in a large pot of boiling water according to package directions. Drain, cool pasta by rinsing with cold running water and drain again. Pour pasta into a large bowl; add red onion, celery, bell pepper, capers, Parmesan, salmon and pine nuts (if using). Pour on dressing and toss until well combined. Chill until time to serve.

Serves 4 to 6

Blackened Salmon Caesar Salad

  1 head romaine lettuce
  1 tablespoon paprika
  $\frac{1}{2}$ teaspoon cayenne pepper
  2 teaspoons onion powder
  2 teaspoons garlic powder
  2 teaspoons brown sugar
  2 teaspoons salt
  $\frac{1}{2}$ teaspoon ground black pepper
  $\frac{1}{2}$ teaspoon dried thyme
  $\frac{1}{2}$ teaspoon dried oregano
  $\frac{1}{4}$ cup shredded Parmesan cheese
  $\frac{3}{4}$ cup garlic croutons
  $\frac{1}{4}$ cup bottled Caesar salad dressing
  3 tablespoons (about) olive oil
  1 to 1 $\frac{1}{2}$ pounds salmon fillet, skin and bones removed

Trim the romaine, rinse well in cold water and drain. Spread the lettuce leaves out on a strip of paper towels, roll up and place in a plastic bag. Refrigerate at least 1 hour or up to 1 day ahead.

In a small bowl, prepare the blackening spice by combining the paprika, cayenne, onion powder, garlic powder, brown sugar, salt, pepper, thyme and oregano.

Cut fillet into 4 serving pieces. Brush both sides with olive oil then sprinkle with the blackening spice to coat both sides evenly (you won't need all of the mixture; the leftover spice is great on steak or chicken). In a large, heavy skillet (cast iron is best) heat 1 tablespoon olive oil over high heat. Add the salmon and cook until blackened, 3 to 5 minutes. Turn fillets, reduce heat to medium and continue cooking until fish is done and can be easily flaked with a fork.

Cut or tear lettuce into bite-size pieces; place in a large bowl. Add the Parmesan, croutons and salad dressing. Toss to combine, then divide evenly onto 4 plates. Refrigerate while you cook the salmon. To serve, top each salad with a piece of fish, blackened side up.

Serves 4

Salmon on Spinach Salad

4 tablespoons extra virgin olive oil, divided
1 tablespoon rice wine vinegar
$1/2$ teaspoon sugar
$1/4$ teaspoon salt
$1/4$ teaspoon black pepper
2 thick slices of bacon, diced
$1/2$ pound salmon fillet (skin and bones removed), cut
    into $1/2$" to $3/4$" cubes
1 tablespoon all-purpose flour
1 bag (6 ounces) baby spinach
2 large eggs, hardboiled, peeled and chopped
2 large green onions, thinly sliced
1 tablespoon pine nuts or chopped pecans (optional)

Make dressing by mixing 3 tablespoons of the olive oil, the rice wine vinegar, sugar, salt and pepper in a small bowl. Set aside.

In a shallow bowl or pie plate, sprinkle salmon cubes with flour and, using your fingers, toss gently until all sides of cubes are coated lightly with flour.

In a nonstick skillet, cook bacon until crisp; remove with a slotted spoon and drain on paper towels. Pour off all but about 1 tablespoon of bacon drippings in skillet, add remaining 1 tablespoon of olive oil and salmon cubes. Cook over medium-high heat, turning and stirring often to prevent sticking, until salmon is brown and cubes are just cooked through.

Place spinach, cooked bacon, chopped eggs and green onions in a large bowl; toss with dressing. Divide salad onto 2 serving plates. Spoon half of hot cooked salmon cubes over each salad, sprinkle with pine nuts or pecans and serve.

Serves 2

Warm Mediterranean Salmon Salad

If you have trouble getting excited about eating salad in the dead of winter, this hearty, warm salad might change your mind.

$1/2$ cup extra virgin olive oil
1 tablespoon balsamic vinegar
2 tablespoons lemon juice
1 teaspoon salt
$1/2$ teaspoon black pepper
1 cup cooked salmon (about $1/2$ pound) or 1 small can
   (7 to 8 ounces) salmon, skin and bones removed
1 cup couscous
1 medium carrot, grated
1 cup roughly chopped fresh spinach
$1/4$ cup diced red onion
1 $1/2$ cups low-sodium chicken or vegetable broth
1 cup cherry tomatoes, halved
1 cup peeled, diced cucumber
$1/2$ cup sliced pitted olives (Kalamata or large green olives
   are best)

Prepare the dressing by combining the olive oil, balsamic vinegar, lemon juice, salt and pepper in a small bowl. Set aside.

In a large bowl, flake salmon with a fork then combine it with the couscous, carrot, spinach and onions. Place broth in a microwave-safe bowl or glass measuring cup and microwave on high until it just begins to boil (2 to 4 minutes, depending on your microwave).

Carefully pour broth over salmon and couscous mixture; stir well. Immediately cover bowl tightly with foil or plastic wrap and let stand 5 minutes. Remove cover and fluff salad with fork. Stir in tomatoes, cucumber, olives and prepared dressing. Mix well and serve while still warm.

Serves 4

Butternut Squash Soup with Salmon Croutons

1 medium butternut squash (2 to 2 ½ pounds)
1 medium onion, chopped (about 1 cup)
3 tablespoons butter or margarine
2 cups chicken or vegetable broth
8 (about) large, fresh sage leaves, whole
1 teaspoon cumin
¼ teaspoon black pepper
1 cup whole milk
Salt to taste
2 tablespoons vegetable oil
½ pound king salmon fillet, skin and bones removed
1 tablespoon flour
Coarse sea salt

Peel squash and cut in half lengthwise. Using a large spoon, scoop out seeds and discard; cut squash into 1" chunks and set aside.

In a large saucepan, cook the onion in the butter or margarine over medium heat for 5 minutes or until softened. Add the broth, squash chunks, 3 or 4 whole sage leaves, cumin and pepper; increase heat to high and bring to a boil. Reduce heat to low, cover and simmer until the squash is very tender and beginning to fall apart (about 20 to 30 minutes). Remove and discard the sage leaves then transfer the squash mixture carefully to a blender or food processor, in batches, and purée until smooth. Return the puréed soup to the saucepan and stir in milk and salt to taste. Cover and keep warm over low heat.

In a non-stick skillet, heat the vegetable oil over medium-high heat. Cut salmon into ½" cubes and pat dry with paper towels; sprinkle with flour and toss with your fingers to coat on all sides. Add the salmon to the skillet and cook, stirring, until the cubes are browned around the edges and just cooked through (about 3 minutes).

Ladle hot soup into serving bowls. Place about ¼ cup of salmon cubes in the center of each bowl. Garnish each with a sage leaf and a pinch of sea salt.

Serves 4

Easy Salmon Bouillabaisse

Traditionally, bouillabaisse *is a fisherman's stew made with a mix of whatever fish and shellfish were available from that day's catch. Although this quick and easy version uses only salmon, it still has all the flavor of the original. Serve with crusty bread to soak up the broth.*

2 tablespoons vegetable oil
1 medium yellow onion, diced
1 stalk celery, thinly sliced
2 large cloves garlic, minced or pressed
1 tablespoon tomato paste
2 bottles (8 ounces each) clam juice
3 cups low-sodium chicken or vegetable broth
2 large tomatoes, peeled and coarsley chopped
1 teaspoon finely minced or zested orange peel, orange part only (optional)
1 teaspoon fennel seed
Pinch of saffron threads crumbled into 1 tablespoon hot water
Salt and pepper to taste
1 ½ pounds salmon fillet (skin and bones removed), cut into 4 serving pieces
2 tablespoons parsley, chopped

In a small Dutch oven sauté onion and celery in oil over medium heat until softened, about 5 minutes. Add garlic and tomato paste and cook, stirring, for another minute. Stir in clam juice and broth then add chopped tomato, orange peel (if using), fennel seed and saffron/water mixture. Bring broth to a boil then reduce heat to low. Taste and add salt and pepper if needed.

Carefully place salmon pieces into broth. Cover and simmer until fish is done, 8 to 10 minutes depending on thickness. (If fish is not completely submerged, carefully turn pieces over about halfway through cooking time.)

Place a piece of fish in each of 4 shallow soup bowls. Ladle broth over the fish, sprinkle with parsley and serve.

Serves 4

Salmon and Corn Chowder

> 3 thick slices bacon, diced
> 2 tablespoons butter
> 2 medium potatoes (about 1 pound), peeled and cut into
>   1" chunks
> $\frac{1}{2}$ cup yellow onion, diced
> 3 cups chicken or vegetable broth
> $\frac{1}{4}$ teaspoon to 1 teaspoon Tabasco sauce (to taste)
> 1 teaspoon fresh thyme leaves
> 2 tablespoons cornstarch mixed in $\frac{1}{4}$ cup cold water
> 1 $\frac{1}{2}$ cups half-and-half
> 2 cups fresh or frozen corn kernels
> 1 $\frac{1}{2}$ cups cooked salmon (about $\frac{3}{4}$ pound), skin and
>   bones removed
> Salt and black pepper

Cook bacon in a small (4- to 5-quart) Dutch oven over medium heat until it's crisp. Remove with a slotted spoon, drain on paper towels and set aside. Add the butter to the bacon drippings, then add potato and onion. Cook, stirring often, for about 10 minutes or until potatoes are almost done. Add the broth, Tabasco and thyme and bring to a boil; reduce heat and simmer for 5 to 10 minutes or until potatoes are done. Whisk in the cornstarch and water mixture and cook, stirring, until the soup thickens and is smooth.

Stir the reserved bacon, the corn and the half-and-half into the chowder, then gently stir in the salmon, breaking the fish up into large chunks. Let cook for 1 to 2 minutes, until all ingredients are heated through. Taste and season with salt and pepper if necessary.

Serves 4

King Salmon Steamed in Paper
with Arugula Pesto

Chef Al Levinsohn
Kincaid Grill, Anchorage

4 king salmon fillets, about 6 ounces each
1/2 cup julienne leeks
1/2 cup julienne carrots
1/2 cup julienne celery
1/2 cup hot house tomato, peeled, seeded and diced
Kosher salt and black pepper to taste
4 teaspoons white wine
Parchment paper
1 egg white, beaten
Arugula Pesto (recipe follows)

Preheat oven to 350°F. In a small bowl, mix leeks, carrots, celery and tomato. Season salmon fillets with salt and pepper.

Cut 4 large pieces of parchment paper into heart shapes, being sure to leave enough extra room for folding edges closed. On one side of each heart place a small bed of the mixed vegetables. Top with a seasoned salmon fillet, skin side down. Spoon remaining vegetables on top of fish and drizzle each fillet with a teaspoon of white wine.

Brush egg white around the edge of the parchment. Fold paper closed over fish and make small tight folds all around the edges, until a package is formed. Place sealed packages on a baking sheet and cook for 15 to 18 minutes or until the paper has puffed. Place packages on plates and serve immediately, cutting open at the table. Serve with Arugula Pesto.

Serves 4

Kincaid Grill Arugula Pesto

1 cup arugula, cleaned
1 teaspoon minced garlic
¼ cup grated parmesan cheese
¼ cup toasted pine nuts
½ cup (about) olive oil
Salt and pepper to taste

Place arugula, garlic, parmesan and pine nuts in bowl of food processor. Pulse a few times until combined. With processor running, stream in olive oil until pesto reaches desired consistency. Season with salt and pepper to taste.

Makes about 1½ cups.

Main Courses

World's Simplest Salmon

When you're lucky enough to have salmon fresh from the water, its flavor speaks for itself and this simple preparation is really all that's needed.

1 ½ to 2 pounds fresh salmon fillet, cut into 4 pieces
Extra virgin olive oil
Salt
Black pepper

Preheat oven to 500°F.

Line a large, rimmed sheet pan with aluminum foil. Brush the foil with olive oil and arrange the salmon on it, skin side down, leaving at least 2" between pieces. Brush the pieces lightly with oil then season with salt and pepper. Place fish in oven, immediately reduce heat to 450° and cook for 8 to 12 minutes (depending on thickness of fillet), without turning, until fish is just done in the center.

Serves 4

Basic Poached Salmon

    6 to 8 sprigs of fresh dill
    12 whole black peppercorns
    3 or 4 slices of lemon
    1 pound salmon fillet (skin on), cut into 2 pieces

Fill a large, deep skillet half full of water. Add dill, peppercorns and lemon slices and bring to a boil. Reduce heat to low and carefully add salmon. Add more water if necessary to cover fish. Cover pan and simmer for 6 to 10 minutes, depending on thickness of fillet. Test for doneness by flaking with a fork. When done, carefully remove fish with a spatula and allow to cool.

Makes about 2 cups of chopped or flaked fish.

Basic Steamed Salmon

    6 to 8 sprigs of fresh dill
    3 or 4 slices of lemon
    1 pound salmon fillet (skin on), cut into 2 or 3 pieces to fit
      into steamer

Fit a bamboo steamer (line with a piece of parchment to keep fish skin from sticking to steamer) or steamer rack (spray with cooking spray) into a deep, straight-sided skillet or saucepan. Place about 1" of water in the bottom of pan (water should not touch the bottom of the steamer). Add dill and lemon slices to the water and bring to a boil. Reduce heat to low, arrange the fish in the steamer, cover and simmer for 6 to 10 minutes, depending on thickness of fillet. Test for doneness by flaking with a fork. When done, carefully remove fish with a spatula and allow to cool.

Makes about 2 cups of chopped or flaked fish.

Asian Lacquered Salmon

$3/4$ cup low-sodium soy sauce
$1/2$ cup orange juice or water
1 tablespoon sesame oil
1 tablespoon peeled fresh ginger, finely minced or grated
2 tablespoons Mirin (rice wine) or dry sherry
1 tablespoon brown sugar
1 large garlic clove, finely minced
2 teaspoons cornstarch
1 $1/2$ to 2 pounds salmon fillet (about 1" thick), cut into 4
    equal portions
2 bunches of green onions, ends trimmed

Preheat oven to 400°F. Grease a baking pan (not glass), large
enough to hold salmon fillets without crowding, with vegetable oil
or cooking spray.

Combine soy sauce, orange juice or water, sesame oil, ginger, rice
wine, brown sugar and garlic in a small bowl. Add cornstarch and
whisk until smooth. Set aside.

Remove 2 large green onions, slice thinly on the diagonal and set
aside for garnish. Place remaining green onions (whole) in baking
pan, spreading them out evenly to make a platform for the salmon.
Arrange salmon, skin side down, on top of green onions.

Stir the sauce, then spoon it evenly over the fillets. Bake uncovered
for about 15 to 20 minutes, until the fish is just cooked through,
basting frequently and checking for doneness. If the pan starts
to become dry, add a little water to prevent the green onions and
sauce from burning. Garnish fillets with reserved sliced green
onions.

Serves 4

Broiled Salmon with Herbs

This recipe came from my longtime friend RuthAnn Dickie.

1 ½ to 2 pounds fresh or frozen salmon steaks or skinless
    fillets, about ¾" thick
2 tablespoons finely grated onion
2 tablespoons lemon juice
4 tablespoons melted butter
2 tablespoons olive oil
1 teaspoon salt
¼ teaspoon pepper
2 teaspoons minced marjoram or ½ teaspoon crumbled
    dried marjoram
1 tablespoon minced chives
2 tablespoons minced parsley or watercress

Preheat broiler. Place oven rack so that the pan will be at least 6"
from the heat source.

Wipe the fish with a damp cloth or paper towel and arrange on a
greased broiler pan. Combine all remaining ingredients and spoon
half of the sauce mixture over the fish. Broil for 4 minutes; turn
and pour half of the remaining sauce over the fish. Broil for
4 to 6 minutes longer, or until the fish flakes easily when tested
with a fork.

Remove fish to a hot platter; spoon on remaining sauce and
garnish with additional parsley or watercress.

Serves 4

Honey Mustard Glazed Salmon

1 ½ to 2 pounds salmon fillet (1" to 1 ½" thick)
¼ teaspoon salt
1 garlic clove, minced or pressed
2 tablespoons Dijon mustard
2 teaspoons lemon juice
1 tablespoon honey
¼ teaspoon black pepper

Preheat boiler. Prepare broiler pan by lining with aluminum foil and brushing foil lightly with oil or spraying with cooking spray. Cut salmon into 4 pieces and arrange, skin side down, on pan. Sprinkle lightly with salt.

In a small bowl, mix garlic, mustard, lemon juice, honey and pepper; brush a thin layer of the mixture evenly on top of the salmon pieces. Broil at least 6" from heat until fish is cooked through, 10 to 15 minutes, depending on thickness (do not turn fish over). Watch the fish carefully as it cooks — if the honey begins to burn, move the rack a little farther from the heat.

Serves 4

Salmon with Roasted Garlic

    1 large head of garlic
    3 tablespoons olive oil
    2 tablespoons butter, softened
    1 ½ to 2 pounds salmon fillets, cut into four pieces
    2 teaspoons fresh lemon juice
    Salt and pepper
    2 tablespoons bread crumbs

At least 1 ½ hours or up to 1 day ahead, prepare the roasted garlic purée: Preheat oven to 325°F. Cut about ½" off the top of the head of garlic and place it a small ramekin, custard cup or other ovenproof dish. Pour the olive oil over the garlic and cover the ramekin tightly with foil. Place the covered ramekin into a slightly larger oven-proof dish, cover it with a lid or foil and bake until the garlic is very soft, about 50 to 60 minutes. Remove the dish from the oven, uncover and lift out the head of garlic with a spoon (reserve the oil) and let cool.

When it is cool enough to handle, pick up the head of garlic and squeeze it over a small bowl — the cooked garlic cloves should pop out easily. Discard the remainder of the garlic head. Add 1 tablespoon of the oil from the bottom of the ramekin, the butter and a pinch of salt to the garlic in the bowl. Mash to a smooth paste with a fork. (If the garlic purée is prepared ahead, cover and refrigerate. Bring it to room temperature before proceeding with the recipe.)

Preheat oven to 450°F. Place the salmon pieces, skin side down, on a lightly greased baking sheet. Pat the fish dry with a paper towel then season lightly with salt and pepper. Drizzle each piece with ½ teaspoon lemon juice, spread one-fourth of the garlic purée over each, then sprinkle each piece of fish evenly with about ½ tablespoon of bread crumbs. Bake salmon until just cooked through, about 8 to 12 minutes, depending on thickness.

Serves 4

Salmon Stuffed with Arugula and Feta

> 1 cup arugula or baby spinach, washed and roughly chopped
> ¼ cup feta cheese, crumbled (about 1 ounce)
> 1 tablespoon pine nuts or chopped pecans
> 1 tablespoon extra virgin olive oil
> ¾ pound to 1 pound center-cut salmon fillet, bones removed
>   (at least 1" thick)
> Salt and freshly ground black pepper

Preheat oven to 450°F.

In a small bowl, combine arugula, feta and pine nuts. Drizzle on 2 teaspoons of the oil and mix lightly. Set aside.

Place the fish skin side down on a cutting board. Insert a small, sharp knife into the center of the thickest side of the fillet and cut a deep pocket into it, being careful to leave at least ½" around the other three sides of the fish.

Stuff the arugula mixture into the pocket in the salmon (don't worry if you overfill it a little). Transfer the fish, still skin side down, to a small greased baking pan or pie pan. Brush the top of the fish with the remaining teaspoon of olive oil and season with salt and pepper. Place in preheated oven and bake for 14 to 18 minutes, until fish flakes easily with a fork.

Serves 2

Grilled Salmon with Peaches and Chardonnay

This recipe came from my friend JoAnn Grady, one of Juneau's finest cooks.

> 1 large bag (16 ounces) frozen sliced peaches, thawed overnight in the refrigerator
> 2 tablespoons fresh grated ginger
> 1 teaspoon sugar
> 2 tablespoons lemon juice
> 1 ½ cups (about) dry Chardonnay
> JoAnn's Basil Pesto (recipe on next page)
> 4 large king salmon steaks (3 to 4 pounds total) or 3 to 4 pounds king salmon fillet, cut into 8 serving pieces
> 2 tablespoons olive oil
> 1 tablespoon brown sugar

Early in the day (or the day before serving), empty the bag of thawed peaches and their juices into a bowl. Add, ginger, sugar, lemon juice and just enough Chardonnay to cover peaches. Stir, cover and refrigerate at least 4 hours or overnight.

About an hour before serving, remove peach mixture from refrigerator and let it come up to room temperature. Prepare the pesto and set aside.

Brush the salmon with olive oil and lightly sprinkle with brown sugar. Cook salmon on barbeque grill about 10 to 15 minutes total (depending on thickness), turning once, until fish is cooked through.

To serve: Place cooked fish on a platter. Using a slotted spoon, remove the peaches from the bowl and spoon them over the fish. Pour about ¾ cup of the peach/Chardonnay liquid remaining in the bowl over the fish (serve the remainder of the liquid in a small pitcher with the fish). Top each piece of fish with a dollop of pesto and serve.

Serves 6 to 8

JoAnn's Basil Pesto

$^1/_4$ cup pine nuts
1 large bunch basil, washed, dried and stems removed
4 cloves garlic, peeled
1 to 1 $^1/_4$ cups olive oil
1 to 1 $^1/_2$ cups cups finely grated Parmesan cheese

Toast pine nuts in a dry skillet for about 5 minutes, shaking or stirring frequently and taking care not to burn. Place toasted nuts in a blender or food processor and grind them finely. Pour into a bowl and set aside.

Place basil, garlic and 1 cup of the oil in the blender or food processor. Process until the mixture forms a smooth paste, stopping occasionally to scrape down sides. Pour into the bowl with the ground pine nuts and mix well. Stir in about a cup of the Parmesan. Adjust the consistency of the pesto by adding more olive oil to make it thinner or more cheese to thicken it.

Use the pesto to top the cooked salmon. To keep the remaining pesto, pour a thin layer of olive oil over the surface to prevent discoloring, cover tightly and store in the refrigerator or freezer.

Makes about 2 cups

Citrus Salmon

This simple yet flavorful recipe came from my friend, Susan Sullivan.

    1 whole salmon fillet, 2 to 3 pounds
    Salt and pepper
    1 orange, thinly sliced
    1 lemon, thinly sliced
    1 small onion, thinly sliced

Preheat oven to 400°F or prepare outdoor grill for cooking.

Rinse the salmon fillet, pat dry and place skin side down on a
large sheet of aluminum foil. Season with salt and pepper. Cover
the fish with the slices of orange, lemon and onion. Seal the
foil tightly; place packet on a broiler pan or heavy baking sheet
and place in oven (or place the packet directly on the outdoor
grill). Cooking time will vary depending on the thickness of the
fish, but should be about 30 minutes for a 1" thick fillet. Open the
foil and check for doneness; re-seal and return to oven or grill if
the fish is not done yet.

After cooking, open foil, remove orange, lemon and onion slices
and set aside. To serve, slide the fillet off the skin and place the
fish on a platter. Arrange the orange, lemon and onion slices
around the fish and serve.

Serves 4 to 6

Crispy Salmon Cakes

1 large stalk celery, chopped (about ½ cup)
1 small onion, finely chopped (about ½ cup)
3 tablespoons vegetable oil, divided
1 cup bread crumbs
¾ pound to 1 pound salmon fillet, skin and bones removed
1 large egg, beaten
1 tablespoon mayonnaise
1 tablespoon parsley, finely minced
¼ teaspoon to 1 teaspoon Tabasco sauce (use more or less
   to taste)
¼ teaspoon salt

Heat 1 tablespoon vegetable oil in a large nonstick skillet over medium heat. Add celery and onions; cover and cook, stirring occasionally, until tender and lightly browned (about 5 minutes). Set aside to cool slightly.

Finely chop fish into cubes (approximately ¼") with a knife — do not use a food processor. Place fish in a bowl and add ⅓ cup of the bread crumbs, the sautéed vegetables, egg, mayonnaise, parsley, Tabasco, and salt. Gently mix until all ingredients are well combined.

Pour remaining ⅔ cup bread crumbs onto a sheet of waxed paper. Form the salmon mixture (it will be very soft) into 4 patties about 3" in diameter. Dip patties into bread crumbs, turning and pressing to coat both sides completely. Place patties on a plate and refrigerate for at least 15 minutes.

Wipe skillet clean with a paper towel. Add remaining 2 tablespoons vegetable oil and heat over medium. Cook salmon cakes for 10 to 12 minutes, turning 2 or 3 times, until cakes are golden brown and fish is cooked through.

Serves 2

Salmon Roll-Ups

1 pound salmon fillet (skin and bones removed),
  coarsely chopped
¼ cup bread crumbs
1 egg white
2 tablespoons butter, melted
¼ cup onion, grated or finely minced
2 tablespoons parsley, chopped
1 teaspoon cumin
1 teaspoon chili powder
½ teaspoon salt
¼ teaspoon black pepper
4 large sheets frozen phyllo dough (about 12" by 17"), thawed
Nonstick cooking spray

Preheat oven to 425°F.

In a bowl, mix salmon, bread crumbs, egg white, melted butter, onion, parsley, cumin, chili powder, salt and pepper. Set aside.

Place one sheet of phyllo on a work surface with the long side at the bottom (cover remaining phyllo with a damp towel to keep it from drying out). Spray the phyllo evenly with cooking spray, top with another sheet and spray again. With a sharp knife, cut the phyllo down the middle into two pieces, each approximately 12" by 8".

Spoon one-fourth of the salmon mixture evenly along the bottom edge of one of the phyllo pieces, leaving a 1" border on each side. Fold the sides over the filling then roll the salmon tightly in the phyllo to create a log-shaped roll. Make another roll with the second phyllo piece then, using the remaining two phyllo sheets, repeat the instructions to make two more rolls (make a total of four rolls).

Spray a rimmed baking sheet with cooking spray. Place salmon roll-ups on pan, seam sides down, at least 2" apart and bake for 15 to 20 minutes until golden brown and salmon is cooked through.

Serves 2

Alaska Salmon Quiche

Pastry for 1-crust pie (homemade, frozen or refrigerated)
1 teaspoon vegetable oil
1 ⅓ cups grated Gruyère or Swiss cheese (about 4 ounces)
3 strips bacon, fried crisp and crumbled or ¼ cup finely
    chopped smoked salmon, skin and bones removed
1 ½ cups cooked salmon (about ¾ pound), skin and bones
    removed
3 large green onions, thinly sliced (white and green part)
3 large eggs (do not use egg substitute)
½ cup half-and-half
¾ cup milk
½ teaspoon salt
¼ teaspoon pepper

Preheat oven to 425°F. If using a frozen pie crust, allow it to thaw according to package instructions.

Brush bottom and sides of pie shell with vegetable oil. Scatter half of the cheese, the bacon, salmon (break it into pieces with your fingers), green onions and remaining cheese (in that order) onto the bottom of the pie shell. In a bowl, whisk together eggs, half-and-half, milk, salt and pepper until well blended. Place pie pan on a rimmed baking sheet then slowly pour egg mixture over filling in crust.

Carefully transfer to oven. Bake for 15 minutes at 425°F then reduce temperature to 300°F and continue baking for another 30 to 35 minutes, or until a knife inserted about 1" from the edge comes out clean. Remove quiche from oven and let stand for 15 minutes before cutting.

Serves 4 to 6

Canadian Salmon Pie

This pie is based on the French-Canadian meat pie called tourtiere. *The recipe, adapted from one which originally appeared on cans of pink salmon, has been simplified with several time-saving shortcuts.*

> 1 large baking potato, about 1 pound (or use 1 $\frac{1}{2}$ cups frozen hash brown potatoes, thawed)
> 2 tablespoons butter or margarine
> 1 medium onion, chopped (or use about $\frac{3}{4}$ cup frozen chopped onion, thawed)
> 1 clove garlic, minced or pressed
> $\frac{1}{4}$ cup milk
> 1 teaspoon minced fresh dill or $\frac{1}{2}$ teaspoon dried dill weed (optional)
> $\frac{1}{4}$ teaspoon ground black pepper
> 1 $\frac{1}{2}$ to 2 cups cooked salmon (about 1 pound), skin and bones removed, or 1 large can salmon (14 to 15 ounces), drained well, skin and bones removed if desired
> Pastry for 2-crust pie (homemade, frozen or refrigerated)

Preheat oven to 425°F. If using a frozen pie crust, allow it to thaw according to package instructions.

If using a raw potato, peel potato and cut into $\frac{1}{2}$" cubes. Place in a saucepan and cover with water. Bring to a boil and cook about 10 minutes, or until almost done (potato should still be firm). Drain.

In a large skillet over medium-high heat, melt butter and add onions. Cook until soft and golden, about 5 minutes. Add garlic and cook 1 minute longer. Remove from heat and gently stir in potatoes, milk, dill, pepper and salmon. Spoon filling into pastry-lined pie pan. Cover with top crust, trim pastry around edges and crimp with tines of a fork to seal. Cut 3 or 4 small slits in top crust to vent steam.

Bake on rack in lowest third of oven until top is golden brown, 30 to 35 minutes. Can be served hot or cold (to serve cold, allow baked pie to cool, then cover and chill).

Serves 4 to 6

Russian Salmon Pie

This is a simple version of classic Coulibiac, *a fussy dish described in* Escoffier's A Guide to Modern Cookery *(1909) as made with salmon or sturgeon, onion, mushrooms, rice, whole hardboiled eggs and* vesiga *(spinal marrow of the sturgeon) then wrapped in puff pastry and baked. This easy recipe came from my friend Cass Crandall.*

> Pastry for 2-crust pie (homemade, frozen or refrigerated)
> 1 ½ cups cooked rice
> 1 ½ to 2 cups cooked salmon (about 1 pound), skin and bones removed, or 1 large can salmon (14 to 15 ounces), drained well, skin and bones removed if desired
> Salt and pepper to taste
> 1 large yellow onion, very thinly sliced
> 1 cup finely shredded cabbage (optional; see note)
> 2 large eggs, hardboiled and chopped
> 2 tablespoons butter

Preheat oven to 400°F. If using a frozen pie crust, allow it to thaw according to package instructions.

Put half of the rice into a 9" pie pan lined with pastry. Place the fish on the rice; season with salt and pepper. Top with the onions, then the cabbage, the chopped eggs and finally the remaining rice. Dot with butter and cover with remaining pastry. Cut 3 or 4 slits in the top crust to permit steam to escape. Bake for 30 to 40 minutes, until top is golden brown.

Serves 4 to 6

NOTE: If omitting the cabbage, sprinkle the filling with 2 tablespoons of white wine, chicken or vegetable broth or water before putting on the top crust.

Classic Salmon Loaf

A friend once told me a story about growing up in Southeast Alaska during the Depression: When his family was lucky enough to get a whole salmon, they wasted nothing. After the fillets had been cut off, his mother roasted the fish carcass in a hot oven. Once it was cooked and cooled, my friend's job was picking the bones for every morsel of fish, which his mother then used to make another meal, a salmon loaf. This recipe is a bit fancier than the one my friend's mother used — he said the only essentials in those days were the salmon, some type of crumbs and eggs; any other ingredients were a luxury.

    1 tablespoon vegetable oil
    $\frac{1}{2}$ cup finely diced onions
    $\frac{1}{2}$ cup finely diced celery
    2 large eggs
    $\frac{1}{2}$ cup milk
    1 cup soft bread crumbs or finely crushed saltine crackers (about 18 2" by 2" crackers)
    3 cups cooked salmon (about 1 $\frac{1}{2}$ pounds), skin and bones removed
    1 tablespoon lemon juice
    1 tablespoon chopped fresh parsley
    1 teaspoon chopped fresh dill or $\frac{1}{2}$ teaspoon dry dill weed
    $\frac{1}{2}$ teaspoon salt (omit if using crushed saltines)
    $\frac{1}{4}$ teaspoon ground black pepper

Preheat oven at 350°F.

Heat vegetable oil in small skillet over medium heat. Sauté onions and celery for about 5 minutes, until soft.

In a large bowl, beat eggs with milk until combined. Stir in bread or cracker crumbs, then salmon, sautéed onion and celery, lemon juice, parsley, dill, salt and pepper and mix until well combined. Spoon mixture into a greased loaf pan (9" by 5" by 3") and bake for 40 to 45 minutes. Let stand for 10 minutes before cutting.

Serves 3 to 4

Salmon and Potato Croquettes

1 large potato (about 1 pound)
3 tablespoons butter, softened to room temperature
$\frac{1}{2}$ cup milk
$\frac{1}{2}$ teaspoon salt
$\frac{1}{4}$ teaspoon black pepper
$\frac{1}{2}$ teaspoon Tabasco sauce
$\frac{1}{4}$ cup finely diced red or yellow onion
2 cups cooked salmon (about 1 pound), skin and bones removed
2 large eggs
1 $\frac{1}{2}$ cups soft bread crumbs
$\frac{1}{2}$ cup all-purpose flour
1 quart vegetable oil, for frying

Peel potato and cut into 1" chunks. Place in a saucepan, cover with water and cook until fork tender. Drain potatoes and mash with butter and milk until creamy. Add salt, pepper, Tabasco and onion, then stir in salmon, breaking it up with a fork and mixing until ingredients are well combined. Let cool slightly, then form mixture into golf ball-sized balls.

Beat the eggs with 1 tablespoon water in a shallow bowl. Place bread crumbs and flour in two other bowls. Roll croquettes first in flour, then in egg, then in bread crumbs. Place crumb-coated croquettes on a plate and refrigerate for at least 15 minutes and up to 2 hours.

Heat the oil to 350°F (use a deep frying thermometer) in a deep fryer, large (at least 4-quart) saucepan or Dutch oven. Gently lower croquettes into oil and fry a few at a time (do not crowd pan) until golden brown, turning as needed. Remove and drain on paper towels before serving.

Serves 4

Creamed Salmon in Pastry Shells

1 package frozen puff pastry shells (6 shells)
1 large or 2 medium shallots, thinly sliced
3 tablespoons butter or margarine
3 tablespoons flour
1 tablespoon Dijon mustard
1 cup chicken or vegetable broth
1 cup milk
$\frac{1}{2}$ teaspoon salt
1 teaspoon minced fresh dill or $\frac{1}{2}$ teaspoon dry dill weed
2 cups cooked salmon (skin and bones removed), cut into
$\frac{1}{2}$" cubes
1 tablespoon finely chopped flat leaf parsley

Bake puff pastry shells according to package directions and place on rack to cool.

Melt butter or margarine in a medium saucepan. Add shallot and cook over medium heat for about 2 minutes. Mix in flour and cook another 2 minutes, stirring constantly. Whisk in mustard, broth and milk. Continue cooking over medium heat, stirring often, until mixture thickens and comes to a boil. Stir in salt and dill, then gently fold in salmon. Reduce heat to low and simmer for 2 to 3 minutes, until salmon is heated through. Spoon mixture into baked pastry shells (don't worry if some overflows). Sprinkle parsley over the tops and serve.

Serves 2 to 3

Creamy Mac and Salmon

2 cups (about 8 ounces) large elbow macaroni
1 1/2 teaspoons salt, divided
3 tablespoons butter or margarine
3 tablespoons all-purpose flour
3 cups milk (for a richer dish, use 2 cups milk and 1 cup
    half-and-half)
3 cups shredded sharp Cheddar cheese
1/8 teaspoon cayenne pepper or 1/2 teaspoon Tabasco sauce
1 small can salmon (7 to 8 ounces), drained, skin and bones
    removed if desired
2 slices stale bread, grated or finely chopped to make crumbs
    (or use 1/2 cup prepared bread crumbs)

Preheat oven to 350°F. Grease a 2- to 3-quart casserole.

In a large saucepan, bring 2 quarts of water to a boil. Add macaroni
and 1 teaspoon salt; return to a boil and cook about 8 minutes, until
macaroni is just done. Drain.

Wipe out saucepan and return it to the stove. Melt butter or
magarine over medium heat, add flour and stir until smooth. Cook
about 2 minutes, stirring to prevent browning. Slowly pour in milk
and cook, stirring almost constantly, until sauce thickens and just
comes to a boil (keep heat at medium or lower to prevent bottom
from scorching). Remove pan from heat and add 2 cups of the
cheese, the remaining 1/2 teaspoon salt and the cayenne or Tabasco.
Stir until cheese melts. Mix in drained macaroni then gently fold
in salmon. Pour into greased casserole. Evenly sprinkle with
remaining 1 cup of cheese and top with bread crumbs. Bake for
approximately 30 minutes, until bubbly and top is golden brown.
Let cool for 10 minutes before serving.

Serves 4

Kedgeree

Kedgeree is a British version of a traditional Indian breakfast dish containing lentils, rice, hardboiled eggs and raisins. This Americanized version makes a quick, simple dinner. In case you're tempted to leave out the raisins — don't. Not only are they part of the traditional recipe, they're a perfect complement to the rich curry flavor.

> 4 tablespoons butter, divided
> 1 small onion, diced
> 3 tablespoons flour
> 2 teaspoons curry powder (or more to taste)
> 2 cups whole milk
> ½ teaspoon salt
> 1 ½ cups cooked rice
> ¼ cup golden raisins
> 4 large eggs, hardboiled, peeled and coarsely chopped
> 1 small can salmon (7 to 8 ounces), drained, skin and bones
>   removed if desired

Preheat oven to 350°F.

Melt 1 tablespoon butter in a large saucepan. Add onion and cook about 5 minutes, until it just begins to soften. Remove to a small bowl and set aside. Add remaining butter to saucepan, stir in flour and curry powder and cook about 1 minute. Slowly add milk and cook, stirring constantly, until mixture thickens and almost comes to a boil.

Remove pan from heat. Add rice, raisins, chopped eggs, salmon and cooked onions. Stir gently until combined and pour into a small (2-quart) casserole sprayed with cooking spray.

Bake for 20 to 30 minutes, until hot and bubbly.

Serves 3 to 4

Salmon Fettucine Alfredo

1 pound salmon fillet
2 tablespoons butter
1 large or 2 small shallots, minced
1 cup heavy cream
1 cup finely grated Parmesan cheese
Salt
Freshly ground black pepper
1 package (16 ounces) fettucine
2 tablespoons chopped parsley for garnish

Poach or steam salmon (see basic directions on page 46). Remove skin and bones and break fish up into chunks. Loosely cover with foil to keep warm.

Melt butter in a heavy saucepan over medium heat. Add shallots and cook, stirring, about 2 minutes. Pour in heavy cream, raise heat slightly and slowly bring just to a boil. Reduce heat to low and simmer until sauce has reduced slightly, about 5 minutes. Remove pan from the heat. Whisk in cheese, mixing until thoroughly combined. Season to taste with salt and pepper.

In the meantime, cook pasta in a large pot of boiling water according to package directions. Drain and pour into a serving bowl. Scatter chunked salmon on top; pour sauce over and toss gently to mix. Garnish with chopped parsley; pass additional Parmesan cheese, if desired.

Serves 4

Salmon and Vegetable Lasagna

3 tablespoons olive oil
1 large yellow onion, peeled, halved and thinly sliced
1 red bell pepper, seeds and ribs removed, halved and
    thinly sliced
1 cup carrots, coarsely shredded or thinly sliced
3 cups baby spinach leaves, washed and patted dry
3 cups cooked salmon (about 1 ½ pounds) skin and bones
    removed
2 garlic cloves, minced or pressed
3 tablespoons butter or margarine
¼ cup all-purpose flour
3 cups milk
¾ cup finely grated Parmesan cheese, divided
1 teaspoon salt
½ teaspoon black pepper
1 teaspoon dried thyme
1 teaspoon dried oregano
Pinch of nutmeg
6 to 9 no-boil lasagna noodles (enough to make 3 layers in pan)
1 ½ cups mozzarella cheese, grated
1 large or 2 medium tomatoes, coarsely chopped and drained
    on paper towels

Preheat oven to 400°F.

In a large skillet, heat olive oil over medium heat. Add sliced onions, red pepper and carrots and sauté until vegetables soften, about 10 minutes, stirring occasionally. Add spinach leaves and stir just until wilted, then gently mix in salmon, breaking it up into flakes. Remove from heat and set aside.

In the meantime, melt butter or margarine in a medium saucepan over medium heat; add garlic and cook for about 1 minute. Add the flour and cook, stirring, for about 2 minutes, then slowly mix in milk. Cook, stirring constantly, until sauce thickens and just comes to a boil. Remove sauce from heat and stir in ½ cup of Parmesan, salt, pepper, thyme, oregano and nutmeg.

(continued on next page)

Soak no-boil lasagna noodles in a dish of hot water until they begin to soften, about 10 minutes.

To assemble: Spray a 9" square baking dish with cooking spray. Spoon in 3/4 cup of sauce and place 2 or 3 no-boil noodles on top of sauce. Layer half of the salmon-vegetable mixture, 3/4 cup sauce, 1/2 cup mozzarella and 2 or 3 more noodles. Spread the chopped tomatoes evenly over the noodles, then repeat the layer once more — salmon mixture, sauce, mozzarella and ending with 2 or 3 noodles. Top with remaining sauce, 1/2 cup mozzarella and 1/4 cup Parmesan.

Bake 20 to 30 minutes, or until golden brown and bubbly. Let lasagna stand at least 15 minutes before serving.

Serves 4 to 6

Salmon and Mushroom Linguine

>   4 tablespoons olive oil, divided
>   1 pound mixed fresh mushrooms (such as white, cremini or
>   shiitake), cleaned, stems trimmed and discarded, and sliced
>   ¼ teaspoon crushed red pepper flakes
>   ½ teaspoon salt
>   ½ teaspoon fresh ground black pepper
>   3 large garlic cloves, minced
>   ¾ cup dry white wine or chicken or vegetable broth
>   1 pound salmon fillet (skin and bones removed), cut into
>   ¾" cubes
>   1 package (16 ounces) linguine
>   ¼ cup flatleaf parsley, chopped
>   Grated Parmesan cheese

Heat 2 tablespoons oil over medium-high heat in a large, nonstick
skillet. Add mushrooms, red pepper flakes, salt and pepper and
sauté until cooked and mushrooms begin to release their juices,
8 to 10 minutes. Transfer mixture to a bowl and set aside.

Heat remaining 2 tablespoons oil over medium heat in skillet; add
garlic and sauté for 1 to 2 minutes. Add salmon to pan and cook,
stirring once or twice, for another 3 or 4 minutes. Add wine or
broth to salmon in pan. Reduce heat to low and cook for about 3
minutes, or until fish is just done, stirring gently several times.
Return mushrooms to pan and cook until heated through, about
1 to 2 minutes.

Meanwhile, cook linguine in a large pot of boiling salted water
according to package directions until just tender. Drain pasta well
and pour into a large bowl.

Spoon mushroom and salmon mixture over the pasta. Sprinkle with
parsley and serve with Parmesan cheese.

Serves 4

Quick Salmon Tacos

   2 cups cooked salmon (about 1 pound) skin and bones
      removed
   1 cup canned black beans, drained and rinsed
   3/4 cup salsa (bottled or fresh)
   3 tablespoons fresh cilantro, coarsely chopped
   1 cup fresh tomato, diced
   2 cups shredded iceberg lettuce
   1 cup Cheddar cheese, shredded
   8 ready-to-use taco shells
   Sour cream (for serving)
   Additional salsa (for serving)

Cut or flake salmon into 1/2" to 3/4" pieces and combine it with
the black beans and salsa in a medium skillet. Cook over medium
heat, stirring gently until mixture is just heated through, 3 to 5
minutes. Remove from heat, add cilantro and set aside.

Just before serving, warm the taco shells by placing them on a
large microwave-safe plate and microwaving on high power for
1 to 1 1/2 minutes (or place the shells on a baking sheet and warm
in a preheated 300°F oven for 6 to 8 minutes).

To serve, spoon the salmon mixture into the bottom of the taco
shell. Top with tomato, lettuce, cheese and remaining cilantro.
Serve with sour cream and additional salsa if desired.

Serves 4

Salmon Chili with Beans

    1 tablespoon vegetable oil
    1 medium yellow or red onion, diced
    $\frac{1}{2}$ teaspoon sugar
    2 cans (14 to 15 ounces) diced tomatoes in juice
    2 to 4 teaspoons chili powder, according to taste
    1 teaspoon ground cumin
    2 cans (15 ounces) black, kidney or pinto beans (or a
       combination), drained (reserve about ½ cup of bean
       liquid) and rinsed
    1 can (11 ounces) corn kernels, drained, or 1 cup frozen
       corn kernels
    1 large can salmon (14 to 15 ounces), drained, skin and
       bones removed if desired
    $\frac{1}{4}$ cup sharp Cheddar cheese, shredded (for serving)
    $\frac{1}{4}$ cup sour cream (for serving)
    2 tablespoons chopped cilantro (for serving)

Heat oil in a Dutch oven over medium heat. Add onion, sprinkle with sugar and cook, stirring occasionally, until onion is soft and golden brown (about 5 minutes). Stir in tomatoes, chili powder and cumin, then add beans and corn. Mix well, reduce heat and simmer, uncovered, for about 20 to 30 minutes, until chili begins to thicken (add some of the reserved bean liquid if chili becomes too dry). Add salmon, breaking it up into chunks. Stir gently and simmer for about 5 minutes to heat through.

Spoon into bowls and top each with some cheese, a dollop of sour cream and a sprinkle of cilantro.

Serves 4 to 6

Salmon Tortilla Pie

3 large eggs (or 1 cup egg substitute, such as Eggbeaters)
1 cup milk
1/3 cup all-purpose flour
1 teaspoon baking powder
1 large (10" or "burrito size") flour tortilla
2 cups cooked salmon (about 1 pound) skin and bones
   removed
1/4 cup diced yellow onion
2 tablespoons minced cilantro or flatleaf parsley
1 small (4-ounce) can mild diced green chiles
2 cups shredded Monterey Jack or Pepper Jack cheese
1/2 teaspoon salt
1/2 teaspoon pepper
Sour cream (optional, for serving)
Guacamole (optional, for serving)

Preheat oven to 400°F.

In a small bowl, whisk together eggs or egg substitute, milk, flour and baking powder until ingredients are well combined and no lumps of flour remain.

Grease the bottom and sides of a 9" pie pan with vegetable oil. Press the tortilla into the pan, forming a shell. Brush the inside of the shell with oil or spray with cooking spray. Place the salmon in the shell, breaking it up into chunks. Top with diced onions, cilantro, green chiles, and 1 cup of the cheese. Sprinkle with salt and pepper. Place pie on a rimmed baking sheet then gently pour egg mixture over the filling. Top with the remaining cheese.

Bake on the middle rack in preheated oven for 25 to 30 minutes, until pie is puffy and golden brown and a knife inserted near the center comes out clean. Let pie stand for 10 minutes, then cut into wedges. Serve with sour cream and guacamole if desired.

Serves 4

Easy Salmon Enchiladas

3 cups cooked salmon (about 1 ½ pounds), skin and bones removed
1 can (15 ounces) pinto or black beans, drained and rinsed
½ cup diced red onion
½ cup sliced black olives
4 cups shredded Monterey Jack or sharp Cheddar cheese, divided
1 can (19 ounces) mild or hot enchilada sauce, divided
½ cup sour cream
12 flour tortillas (7" to 8" diameter)

Preheat oven to 375°F. Grease the bottom and sides of a 9" by 13" baking dish.

In a large bowl, coarsely chop the salmon, then combine with the beans, onions, black olives, 2 ½ cups of the cheese and half the can of enchilada sauce (about 1 cup). Mix gently. Spoon a generous ½ cup of filling along the center of a tortilla, roll up and place seam side down in the prepared pan. Repeat with remaining tortillas and filling.

In a small bowl, combine the remaining enchilada sauce and the sour cream, stirring until smooth. Evenly spoon the mixture over the enchiladas, then top with the remaining 1 ½ cups of cheese. Bake for 20 to 25 minutes, until bubbly and browned. Serve with additional sour cream, if desired.

Serves 6 to 8

Teriyaki Fish-Kebabs

1 cup low-sodium soy sauce
$1/4$ cup Mirin (rice wine) or sherry (not cooking sherry)
3 tablespoons vegetable oil
$1/4$ cup brown sugar
2 cloves garlic, finely minced
1 tablespoon peeled and finely minced or grated ginger
$1 1/2$ to 2 pounds salmon fillets (skin and bones removed), at
   least 1" thick, cut into $1 1/2$" chunks
2 bell peppers (1 red and 1 yellow if possible), cut into
   $1 1/2$" pieces
1 large red onion, cut into $1 1/2$" pieces
8 metal or bamboo skewers (if using bamboo, soak skewers
   in a tray of water for 30 minutes before making kebabs)

Preheat broiler to medium high or preheat outdoor grill.

Combine first 6 ingredients in a large zip-top bag, "massaging" with your hands until ingredients are well mixed and brown sugar is dissolved. Set aside for a few minutes to develop flavors.

Prepare salmon and vegetables. Stir marinade and remove ¼ cup to a small bowl and set aside to use for basting. Add salmon chunks and vegetables to remaining marinade in bag, seal and refrigerate for no more than 15 minutes. Drain off marinade and discard. Divide fish and vegetables into 8 equal portions and thread onto the skewers, being careful not to crowd the pieces together.

Place skewers on rack of broiler pan about 6" from heat or on outdoor grill and cook for a total of 15 to 20 minutes, turning 3 or 4 times and basting with reserved marinade.

Serves 4

Thai Salmon Noodles

>1 package (16 ounces) rice noodles, linguine or fettucine
>1 tablespoon sesame oil
>1 tablespoon vegetable oil
>1 large clove of garlic, minced or pressed
>1 pound salmon (skin and bones removed), cut into
>   3/4" to 1" chunks
>2 cups bean sprouts
>1 cup coarsely shredded carrots
>3/4 cup snow peas, cut in half diagonally
>1/2 cup thinly sliced green onions
>Peanut Sauce (recipe follows)
>1/2 cup chopped cilantro
>1/4 cup chopped peanuts

Prepare rice noodles or pasta according to package directions. Drain.

Heat sesame oil and vegetable oil over medium heat in a large skillet. Add garlic and cook for 1 minute, then add salmon and sauté for 3 to 5 minutes, turning gently until fish is almost cooked through. Carefully stir in bean sprouts, carrots, snow peas, green onions and Peanut Sauce and cook for 1 to 2 minutes longer. Pour over noodles or pasta and top with cilantro and chopped peanuts.

Peanut Sauce

>1/4 cup honey
>1/4 cup soy sauce
>1 teaspoon to 1 tablespoon Thai chili paste (see note)
>1/2 cup creamy peanut butter

In small bowl, whisk honey, soy sauce and chili paste. Stir in peanut butter until smooth and well combined. Makes about 1 cup.

Note: Chili pastes vary greatly in heat level. If you are not familiar with the product you are using, start with the smallest amount, taste and add more as needed.

Serves 4

Salmon in Spicy Coconut Sauce

    1 teaspoon vegetable oil
    1 clove garlic, minced or pressed
    1 cup canned coconut milk
    ¼ cup chicken, vegetable or fish stock
    1 teaspoon to 1 tablespoon Thai chili paste (see note on
       page 74)
    1 teaspoon peeled and grated fresh ginger
    ¾ pound salmon fillets (skin and bones removed), cut
       into 2 pieces
    3 green onions, thinly sliced
    Salt and pepper to taste
    Chopped fresh cilantro or parsley (for garnish)
    1 cup cooked Basmati rice (optional)

Heat vegetable oil over medium-high heat in a large, deep skillet or wok. Add the garlic and cook, stirring about 1 minute. Stir in the coconut milk, stock, chili paste and ginger. Bring just to a boil, then reduce the heat to low.

Place the salmon fillets in the pan and spoon some of the sauce over them. Cover and simmer gently for 5 to 8 minutes, or until the fish flakes easily with a fork.

Remove salmon to plates. Stir the green onions into the sauce in the pan; taste the sauce, season with salt and pepper and more chili paste, if needed, and spoon over salmon. Top with chopped cilantro or parsley and serve with Basmati rice if desired.

Serves 2

Wild Alaskan King Salmon with Susitna Valley Hash

Chef Patrick Hoogerhyde
Glacier Brewhouse, Anchorage

4 king salmon fillets, about 6 ounces each
2 tablespoons butter or oil
2 tablespoons birch syrup (maple syrup may be
    substituted)
Chives or scallions, finely chopped
Kosher salt and pepper to taste
Alaskan Alder Smoked Sea Salt Dusted Susitna Valley
    Hash (recipe follows)
8 ounces of fresh greens — arugula, tatsoi (a dark green
    Asian salad green) or wild greens
Smoked Alaskan Porter and Alder Moostard Vinaigrette
    (recipe follows)
Foraged Low Bush Cranberry Infused Birch Syrup
    Molasses (recipe follows)

Heat butter or oil in a sauté pan. Brush salmon with birch syrup, then sprinkle with chives or scallions, salt and pepper. Sear salmon then cook to medium rare (adjust heat as necessary and rotate fish to evenly cook salmon).

To serve: Toss greens in Smoked Alaskan Porter and Alder Moostard Vinaigrette. Place salmon on greens, spoon hash alongside. Drizzle salmon with Foraged Low Bush Cranberry Infused Birch Syrup Molasses.

Serves 4

Alaskan Alder Smoked Sea Salt Dusted Susitna Valley Hash

2 tablespoons butter
1 pound potatoes, diced
½ cup mushrooms, sliced
½ cup onions, diced
Alaskan Alder Smoked Sea Salt (see note on page 78)
    to taste

In a sauté pan, melt butter then add onions and mushrooms and cook until carmelized.

Cook diced potatoes in a deep fryer until crisp and toss with onions and mushrooms. Season to taste with smoked salt.

Smoked Alaskan Porter and Alder Moostard Vinaigrette

2 tablespoons shallots, roughly chopped
1 tablespoon garlic, roughly chopped
1 ½ cups Alder Smoked Moostard stone ground mustard
    (see note on page 78)
¾ cup white wine vinegar
½ to ¾ cup Alaskan Brewing Co. Smoked Porter
2 cups canola oil
Kosher salt to taste

In a food processor or using a hand blender, purée shallots, garlic, mustard and vinegar. Add ½ cup of porter; with processor or blender running, slowly drizzle in oil to emulsify into vinaigrette.

Taste and adjust by adding salt and porter for consistency and desired flavor.

Makes about 4 cups

(continued on next page)

**Foraged Low Bush Cranberry
Infused Birch Syrup Molasses**

2 tablespoons butter
$1/2$ cup shallots, minced
4 tablespoons garlic, minced
$1/2$ cup fireweed honey (local honey may be
   substituted)
2 cups birch syrup (maple syrup may be substituted)
2 tablespoons black peppercorns, cracked
2 cups low bush cranberries

Heat butter in a sauté pan. Add shallots and garlic and cook over low heat until soft. Add honey, syrup and peppercorns and simmer for 3 to 5 minutes. Fold in cranberries and remove from heat.

NOTE: Alaskan Alder Smoked Sea Salt and Alder Smoked Moostard are available in specialty shops in Alaska or on the internet.

Recipe Index

(continued on next page)